I See Rectangles

D.H. Dilkes

Bailey Books
an imprint of
Enslow Publishers, Inc.
40 Industrial Road
Box 398
Berkeley Heights, NJ 07922
USA
http://www.enslow.com

Bailey Books, an imprint of Enslow Publishers, Inc.

Library of Congress Cataloging-in-Publication Data

Dilkes, D. H.
I see rectangles / by D.H. Dilkes.
p. cm. — (All about shapes)
Includes index.
Summary: "Simple text and photographs present a story with a theme about rectangles"—Provided by publisher.
ISBN 978-0-7660-3801-1
1. Rectangles—Juvenile literature. 2. Shapes—Juvenile literature. I. Title.
QA482.D535 2011
516'.154—dc22

2010018402

Paperback ISBN: 978-1-59845-152-8

Printed in the United States of America

052010 Lake Book Manufacturing, Inc., Melrose Park, IL

10 9 8 7 6 5 4 3 2 1

To Our Readers: We have done our best to make sure all Internet Addresses in this book were active and appropriate when we went to press. However, the author and the publisher have no control over and assume no liability for the material available on those Internet sites or on other Web sites they may link to. Any comments or suggestions can be sent by e-mail to comments@enslow.com or to the address on the back cover.

Enslow Publishers, Inc., is committed to printing our books on recycled paper. The paper in every book contains 10% to 30% post-consumer waste (PCW). The cover board on the outside of each book contains 100% PCW. Our goal is to do our part to help young people and the environment too!

Photo Credits: Shutterstock.com

Cover Photo: Shutterstock.com

Note to Parents and Teachers

Help pre-readers get a jumpstart on reading. These lively stories introduce simple concepts with repetition of words and short simple sentences. Photos and illustrations fill the pages with color and effectively enhance the text. Free Educator Guides are available for this series at www.enslow.com. Search for the *All About Shapes* series name.

Contents

Words to Know

books

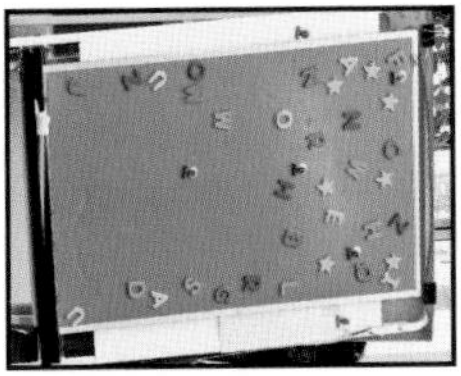

rectangle

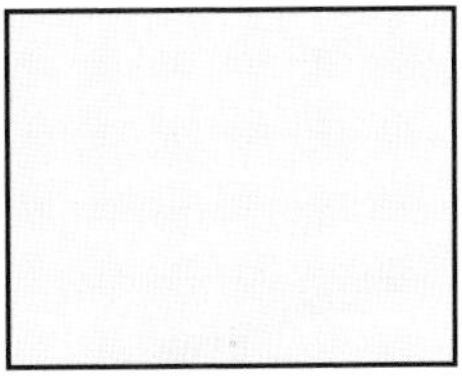

white

LINE
B

I see rectangles

all over school.

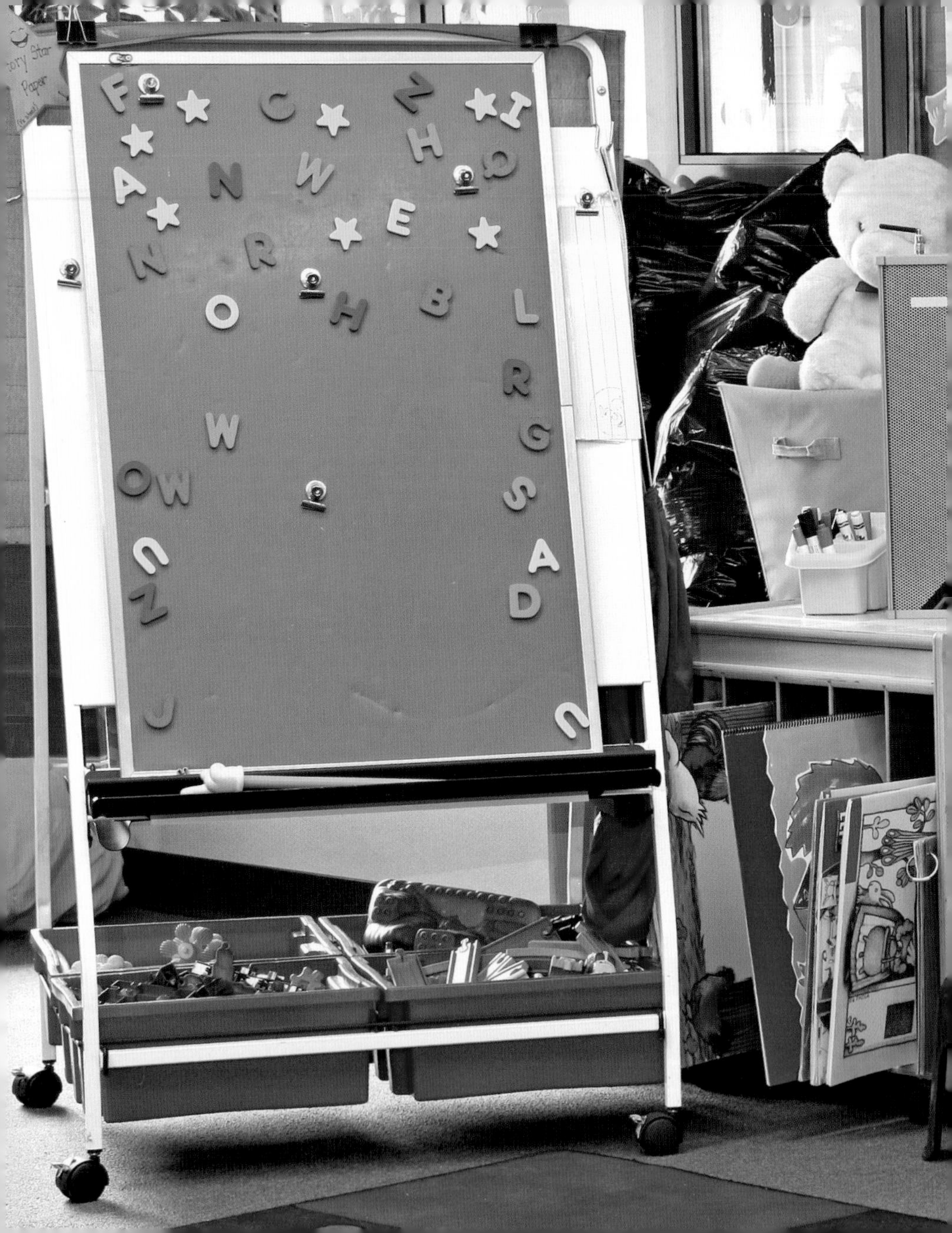

On one I draw.

On one I write.

One to show what I know.

CH3COCOOH

One to keep it white.

In here I put my things

and keep what I eat.

QC1.S
to
QC21.2.S
to
QC173.4.M
QC173.4.M
to
QC174.17
CONTEMPORARY MATHEMATICS

These hold the books

MONTANA
IDAHO
WYOMING
MOUNTAINS
NEVADA
UTAH
COLORADO
ARIZONA
NEW MEXICO
SONORA
NORTHWEST TERRITORIES
YUKON TERRITORY
WISCONSIN
ARKANSAS
MISSISSIPPI
PACIFIC OCEAN

that I read.

Read More

Jones, Christianne C. *Two Short, Two Long: A Book About Rectangles.* Minneapolis, Minn.: Picture Window Books, 2006.

Olson, Nathan. *Rectangles Around Town.* Mankato, Minn. Capstone Press, 2007.

Web Sites

Fisher-Price. *Learn Your Colors and Shapes.*
<http://www.fisher-price.com/us/fun/games/colorshapes/>
Press any key to start!

Kids Learning Station. *Preschool Shapes Worksheets.*
<http://www.kidslearningstation.com/preschool/shapes-worksheets.asp>
Click on "Rectangles Worksheet."

Index

Guided Reading Level: B
Guided Reading Leveling System is based on the guidelines recommended by Fountas and Pinnell.

Word Count: 43